AF430849

ISBN: 979-8-218-88306-5

Library of Congress Control Number: 2026904371

Cover and artwork by Brian Parker, Parker Designs.
Book layout by Johnson Desktop Publishing.

Printed by Cognito Music in the United States of America.

First printing edition 2026.

Examining Transmutations in Standard and Jazz Compositions

By Roger Spencer

Edited By Liz Johnson

Dedicated to my partner in song:

Beegie Adair

FOREWARD

For generations, jazz music has been passed along not only through written scores but also through recordings, performances, mentorship, and—most importantly—listening. This rich diversity of learning modalities is also what makes jazz challenging. Over time, melodies change (or morph), harmonies shift, and interpretations become codified in ways that may or may not reflect the composer's original intent. As performers and educators, we inherit both the beauty and ambiguity of this process.

In this book, Roger Spencer—a veteran bassist and educator in the Los Angeles and Nashville music scenes—addresses the ambiguity surrounding some of the most frequently played and often misinterpreted jazz standards. He approaches each piece with clarity, rigor, and deep respect for the tradition. Beyond serving as a resource for specific works of repertoire, this book provides readers with tools for exploring other pieces in the same manner. By understanding what was written, what has become customary, and where those paths diverge, players gain the freedom to interpret with intention rather than habit. This is essential if we, as performers and educators, are to continue pursuing depth of knowledge of standards old and new.

Roger Spencer brings an exceptional breadth of experience to this work. As a professional jazz bassist, he has spent decades performing with major artists, ensembles, and vocalists, developing a firsthand understanding of how these tunes function in real musical situations—on bandstands, in studios, and in rehearsals. His career has required him to navigate the very issues this book addresses: conflicting lead sheets, evolving "standard" practices, and moments when musicians discover—sometimes mid-performance—that they are not all playing the same version of a tune.

Equally important is the author's long career as an educator. He has taught generations of students at Vanderbilt University, instructing courses in jazz bass, theory, improvisation, and jazz ensembles. As a co-founder of the Nashville Jazz Workshop, he has played a central role in building one of the country's most respected community-based jazz education organizations—an environment where professionals, students, and enthusiasts learn side by side, and where questions of repertoire, tradition, and interpretation naturally arise.

What sets this book apart is the author's ability to connect performance experience with careful scholarship. His analyses are grounded in extensive listening to early recordings, close attention to original sources, and a deep awareness of how melody, lyrics, and harmony interact. He understands that small details—a single melody note, a substituted chord, a shifted cadence—can profoundly affect how a tune feels and functions. At the same time, he recognizes that jazz is a living art form, continually shaped by artists, recordings, and evolving practice.

This text, and the tools it provides, are well-suited for individual practice, private instruction, and classroom use. I am proud to recommend this book and confident that it will enrich the way its readers listen to, think about, and perform jazz repertoire.

Ryan Middagh
Director of Jazz Studies, Vanderbilt University
President, Board of Directors, Nashville Jazz Workshop

About The Author

Originally from Terre Haute, Indiana, Roger Spencer has built an extensive and distinguished musical career spanning decades.

He has performed, traveled, and recorded with legendary big bands including Les Brown and His Band of Renown, Harry James, Ray Conniff, Bill Holman, and Louie Bellson.

His work with renowned jazz artists includes Eddie "Lockjaw" Davis, Buddy DeFranco, Carl Fontana, Sam Butera and the Witnesses, Pete Christlieb, Jake Hanna, the Page Cavanaugh Trio with Al Viola, the Bill Perkins Quartet, Sonny Payne, Pete Jolly, and Alphonse Mouzon.

Roger has also performed with celebrated vocalists such as Rosemary Clooney, Tony Bennett, Peggy Lee, Barbara Cook, Herb Jeffries, Sammy Davis, Jr., Bernadette Peters, and Kevin Mahogany.

Roger earned his Bachelor of Music Education degree from Indiana State University and studied Jazz Studies under the renowned David Baker at Indiana University. He then spent 13 years in Los Angeles, playing on records, doing TV and film recording, and working jazz clubs, with side trips for work to Lake Tahoe and Las Vegas. In 1988, he relocated to Nashville where he soon became an in-demand recording and jazz bassist.

Throughout his Nashville career, Roger has been a driving force in the city's jazz scene. As bassist for the acclaimed Beegie Adair Trio for over 30 years, Roger recorded more than 35 projects with the trio. These recordings became iconic and led the trio to perform at prestigious venues including Carnegie Hall, Birdland, Cotton Club in Tokyo, Pizza Express in London, and Steinway Galleries across the United States.

In 1998, Roger, with his wife Lori Mechem, co-founded Nashville's first jazz school, the Nashville Jazz Workshop, serving as Artistic Director for 27 years. He dedicated himself to nurturing the next generation of jazz musicians and fostering the local jazz community, mentoring countless up-and-coming students and helping them get their start in the business, contributing to broadening Nashville's Music City reputation beyond its country music roots.

Roger's commitment to jazz education extended beyond the Workshop through his 21-year tenure on the faculty at Vanderbilt University's Blair School of Music. There, he taught jazz theory and improvisation, provided private bass instruction, and led numerous combos, further cementing his role as a cornerstone of Nashville's jazz education community.

Roger continues to perform and record while maintaining his commitment to jazz education and performance in Nashville.

INTRODUCTION

In the fall of 1975, I moved to Los Angeles after graduating from college in Indiana and living a year in Boston. I was networking to meet as many players as possible by attending rehearsals and jam sessions. I was invited to a jam session with some of the younger players in town. During that session, someone called the tune "Four". No problem. I knew the tune from the 1960 Miles Davis album, *Workin'*. They counted it off and we began to play. When we got to bar 3, the piano player played Bb-7, Eb7, AbMaj7. This is not an unworkable substitution, but the original changes there are Eb-7, Ab7, F-7. I heard what he played, so I played his chords for the rest of the tune. When we finished, I asked him about the chords he used starting in bar three, and he pointed to those bars in the Real Book he was reading from. That was when I realized that misconceptions of tunes were becoming codified and that those mistakes were gradually becoming standard usage for some players.

No doubt you have run across these conflicts in your playing situations. You learned a tune from whatever source (record, lead sheet, other players), then you're playing the tune with different players and they play something that doesn't agree with your idea of how the tune goes. The conflicts can range from a single melody note or chord change to entire phrases or sections of a tune being left out or played in a different key. This can be very frustrating.

What I'm going to do with this book is look at a number of Great American Songbook and Jazz Standards that are commonly played differently than originally composed and to try to trace the origins of some of these distortions. Some of the ways by which tunes get transformed are: incorrect lead sheets, stylized interpretations by major artists, or unfamiliarity with the details of how tunes were originally composed. We can navigate the minefield of potential conflicts by knowing the tune as it was originally written and knowing the possible alterations that may present themselves. When discussing these transmutations with my students, they often inquire how the tunes became altered by major jazz artists. I wasn't there when these alterations occurred, so all I can offer is conjecture based on who played on the recordings and the chronology of the recorded versions of the tunes.

This book is a result of 50+ years of playing standards and jazz tunes. I learned them from recordings, lead sheets, and, most importantly, on gigs with great pianists and arrangers who knew these tunes and how they were originally composed. I learned to pay attention to what I was hearing for melodies and chord changes and to adjust for different artists' conceptions of these tunes. My job as a bass player is to tie the rhythmic and harmonic elements of the performance together. Knowing how tunes were originally composed and what possible alterations and interpretations may happen, makes it possible for me to help the whole ensemble sound better – more cohesive and refined. To quote Pat Metheny: "The best musicians are not the best players, they're the best listeners."

In the next section of this book, I address a sampling of tunes that I have found problematic during my playing career. The list of 25 tunes is not comprehensive, but the selected tunes are often performed differently by many players. I will contrast and compare lead sheets and recorded versions of these tunes against what I believe to be the composer's original intent.

In the process of researching these tunes, I have isolated several ways that songs get distorted:

1. **Erroneous lead sheets**. The old original *Real Book*, first published illegally in 1975 by two Berklee students, is famous for this. Also be careful using sets of chord changes generated from the iReal Pro app. I warn students to take any lead sheet you find with a grain of salt. Lead sheets are only one person's idea of how the song goes. Unless the lead sheet comes directly from the composer, beware.

2. **Interpreted or arranged versions of tunes on recordings by major artists.** Many great recordings were done before accurate lead sheets were available and sometimes without reference to original artist/composer recordings. Miles Davis frequently recorded tunes as he interpreted (or remembered) them. Example: Miles Davis's version of "In Your Own Sweet Way" was recorded before Dave Brubeck's recording of this tune was released.

3. **Inattention to details.** Composers will write subtle melodic or harmonic differences in "A" sections, or first and second halves of tunes. It is very easy to disregard these differences, particularly if you are not familiar with the lyric.

To get as close as possible to the composer's intent, I have researched numerous recordings of the tunes focusing on the earliest recordings and, when possible, recordings made by the composers themselves. Some of the more contemporary, reliable lead sheets were researched as well. Sources for more reliable lead sheets would include Hal Leonard's copyrighted series of *The Real Book* and the Sher Music *New Real Book* series. Hal Leonard Publishing went through the old, original, Real Book series and corrected most of the blatant errors. Sher Music's *New Real Book* series is informative because it includes alternate chord changes and melodies as reflected by standard usage and well-known performances by major artists.

Another great resource for researching these songs is *The Jazz Discography* by Tom Lord. This discography was valuable to my research for clarifying the chronology of recorded versions of a song, as well as the personnel involved.

Now on to the tunes!

Table of Contents

Song Analyses

All the Things You Are

Composed by Jerome Kern and Oscar Hammerstein II, 1939
Form: A (8 bars) A (8 bars in a different key) B (8 bars) A (12 bars)

This song has a few places where the melody sometimes gets corrupted. The first place is bar 6 in the first A section. Knowledge of the lyric will help remedy this. Note the number of syllables in bar 6:

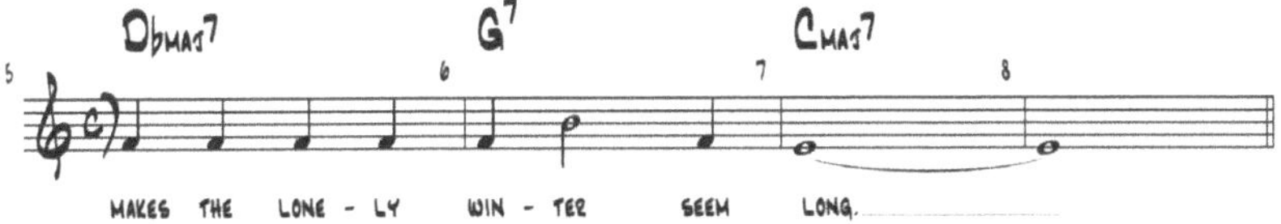

In the second A section, the 6th bar (bar 13 of the song) is different. There are more syllables in the lyric and so, more notes in the melody:

Since the melody here is tied to the lyric, singers will get the first and second A sections right. Instrumentalists not familiar with the lyric will sometimes play bar 6 from the second A section in the first A section as well. This could be because the melodic cadence of the second 8 bars is more climactic and so, more memorable. But that devalues the composer's intent to compositionally develop the ending of the second A section.

The bridge has a couple notes that need attention. In bars 2 and 6, there are a couple chromatic intervals that can be easily misplaced. In bar 2, the note on beat 2 is a half-step pickup into the 9 of the V chord:

In bar 6 of the bridge, the note on beat 2 is a half-step pickup into the root of the V chord:

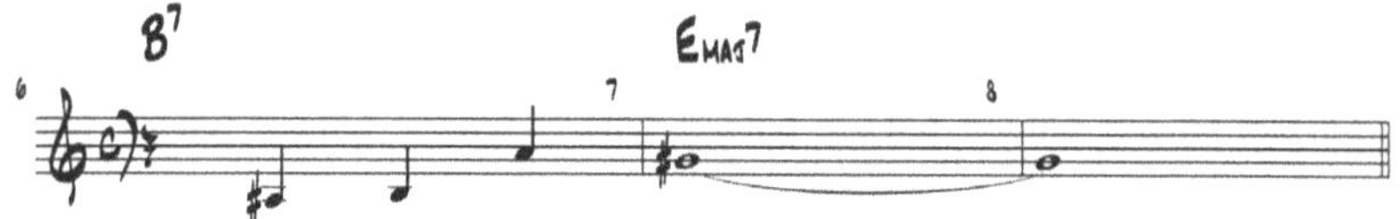

The last A section has an extra 4 bars written in and the ascending arpeggio in bar 9 is often performed incorrectly by both singers and instrumentalists, possibly due to it being written incorrectly in the original *Real Book*. Note that the scale degrees in measure 9 of the last A section of the original composition are: 3 3 5 7.

Last A section in original *Real Book*:

Last A section as written:

Beautiful Love

Composed by Wayne King, Victor Young, and Egbert Van Alstyne
with the lyric by Haven Gillespie, 1931
Form: 32 bars - 16 with first ending, 16 with second ending

I'm including this tune because of one note. You might think I'm being overly fussy, but this is a great example of how one note in the melody, changed by a major artist, can affect how the tune is played from that point forward. The note I'm referring to is the melody note in bar 11 of both halves. In the standard key of D minor, the chord in bar 11 is Bb7. The original melody note in that bar is F. The third phrase of the melody cadences on that F, and then in bar 12 proceeds into the fourth phrase with a pickup starting on E. Then that phrase cadences the first half of the tune on that E.

The versions I've listened to from the '30s, '40s, and '50s perform the melody as written: Bing Crosby, Art Tatum, Benny Carter, George Shearing, Shirley Horn, J.J. Johnson, to name a few.

Then in 1961, Bill Evans recorded the tune for his *Explorations* album. When Bill played the tune, he played an E in bar 11 on the Bb7 chord, making the note a #11. My guess is he did that because he preferred the more dissonant altered sound of the E (Bb7#11) instead of the more diatonic sound of the F (Bb7). That's his judgment call, as he is the artist interpreting the tune the way he wants. But to do that does affect the contour of the melody. The pickup note in bar 12 heading into the fourth phrase is an E. So, the cadence note of the third phrase is the same note as the pickup into the next phrase – not as compositionally sound as the original note in bar 11. Also, if the third phrase cadences on the E, it devalues the E that cadences the fourth phrase. Compositionally, the original melody works better.

After the Bill Evans 1961 recording, most instrumentalists (having learned the tune from this recording) use Bill's E in bar 11. *The Real Book* version also has the E, probably based on the Evans recording. Most vocalists sing the original melody with the F, as they probably studied other vocal recordings to learn the song.

But Not for Me

Composed by George and Ira Gershwin, 1930
Form: 32 bars - 16 with first ending, 16 with second ending

There is some confusion around the first chord of each half of the tune. As written by the Gershwins, the song begins on the I chord. But in practice, many players begin the tune with the II7 chord.

I think this can be traced back to Miles Davis' recordings of the song. Every recording I can find of Miles playing this song begins with the II7 chord. That chord change became codified by the original *Real Book Volume II* which has the tune in the key of F and the chord in the first measure is G7. So, if you learned the tune from Miles or the *Real Book Volume II* you learned it starting on that II7 chord.

The problem with starting on the II7 chord is that it goes against the composer's intent. Gershwin starts the song on the I Major chord. The second four bars of the song restate the same melody as the first four, but Gershwin changed the chord under that melody to the II7 in bar 5. That gives the restatement a freshness and a new direction. When you start with the II7 and repeat the II7 four bars later it devalues Gershwin's compositional intent.

Most vocal arrangements of the tune start with the I Major chord. There are some that dodge the I chord nicely without actually nailing the II7 in bar I. Check out the arrangement Marc Shaiman wrote for Harry Connick's recording of the song for the soundtrack of the movie *When Harry Met Sally*.

Instrumental artists who perform the song beginning with the original I chord include: Ahmad Jamal, Oscar Peterson, Howard Roberts, and Chet Baker.

In this song there is also an issue with the chromatic melody notes in the second 8 bars of each half. Originally those notes were harmonized using passing diminished chords. When improvising over this song, the passing diminished chords can become oppressive to deal with (especially at a brighter tempo) and the chromatic melody notes are no longer there to require those chords. So, in most jazz performances, those chords are usually omitted. If you want insight as to how those chords can work, again refer to Shaiman's arrangement for Harry Connick.

Caravan

**Composed by Juan Tizol, Duke Ellington, and Irving Mills, 1936
Form: A A B A, 8 bars per section
Standard Key: F Minor**

There are a couple of things to be aware of with this tune – the melody in the A sections, and the choice of which bridge to play.

The tune is in F minor, but the first 12 bars of the 16 bar A section are over a static C7b9 chord and the melody is built around the F harmonic minor scale. In bars 11 and 12, most folks play a chromatic scale from the fifth scale degree to the tonic:

Juan Tizol's original melody wasn't completely chromatic, but ended with two whole steps:

I think this is a more exotic sound and is another example of the original composition being superior to what has become standard usage.

The next problem is that there are two commonly used bridges to the tune. If you go back to the first recording of "Caravan", by Barney Bigard and his Jazzopaters (1936), the bridge had no melody. It was a cycle of dominant seventh chords over which the players improvised. The first Duke Ellington recording of the song (May 1937) started with the soloists improvising over the bridge, but on the last bridge of the recording, Duke wrote a sax soli that became the bridge that is most commonly used by vocalists. Here's how it starts:

Check out Billy Eckstine's recording of the tune to hear this vocal bridge.

The July 1937 recording of this tune by Benny Goodman has the Ellington bridge fully developed but also contains an orchestrated lick in the second half of the last bridge that could be the origin of a widely used instrumental bridge. It's the one that starts like this:

Bunny Berrigan's August 1937 recording has this fully developed instrumental bridge.

Come Rain or Come Shine

Composed by Harold Arlen with Lyrics by Johhny Mercer, 1946
From the show St. Louis Woman
Form: 32 bars - 16 with first ending, 16 with second ending

This song is done in many styles and at many tempos. But the puzzle to solve is the chord changes to the last four bars of the first half - measures 13 through 16. There are so many ways to harmonize these measures (some good, some not so good) that there is almost always a train wreck when this tune is called on a gig without a lead sheet. Let's look at some possibilities for these four bars.

The problem begins with trying to understand what Harold Arlen wrote for these four bars. Some early recordings of this tune I studied include:

Ruby Hill, original Broadway cast recording, 1946
Tommy Dorsey with Sy Oliver, 1946
Dick Haymes and Helen Forrest with Earle Hagen, 1946
Jo Stafford with Paul Weston, 1953

When analyzing bars 13 through 16 of these early recordings, the reason for the confusion becomes apparent. The original orchestration of bars 15 and 16 is mostly parallel moving diminished 7th chords with one chord per beat. Here's what's in the publisher's manuscript book of Johnny Mercer tunes:

On the earliest recordings I found of this tune (1946), the rhythm section drops out for measures 15 and 16 leaving a few winds or strings to play the chromatically moving diminished chords. Then the rhythm section comes back in at bar 17 for the second half of the tune. No wonder most players don't know what to play there.

When the Beegie Adair Trio recorded the song, Beegie wanted to honor the one-chord-per-beat harmonic rhythm of bars 15 and 16, but I wanted to have some root movement that was other than chromatic. So, I took the passing diminished chords and converted them to 7b9 chords by adding bass notes that created a more cyclical bass line:

At a brighter tempo, one-chord-per-beat 15th and 16th measures could get a little frantic, so finding a way to thin out the number of chords flying by would be advantageous.

Here's what the original *Real Book* had for those 4 measures:

This relaxes the harmonic meter in bars 15 and 16 by only having two chords per measure. But the two chords per measure in 13 and 14 seem too busy. The original composition has one chord per measure in 13 and 14 and the melody seems to want to settle harmonically in measure 14.

So, after listening to many versions of this tune and trying many ways of playing those four bars, this is what I've settled on:

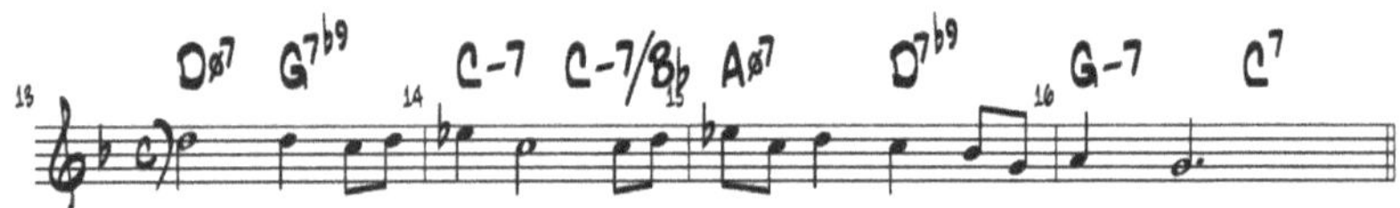

This progression is a compromise of nice harmonic forward motion and root movement with chords that work with the melody.

Other versions you might want to check out are:

Wes Montgomery: *Full House*, 1962
Peggy Lee with Frank DeVol and His Orchestra, 1946
Bill Evans: *Portrait In Jazz*, 1959
Ray Charles: *Genius*, 1959
Art Blakey: *Moanin'*, 1958

Darn That Dream

Composed by Jimmy Van Heusen and Eddie DeLange, 1939.
Form: A A B A, 8 bars per section
Standard Key: G

This tune has a common stylization of the melody and chord changes in bar 6. Here's the melody as played by many artists (from bar 5):

At some point, jazz instrumentalists opted for this approach with the parallel minor 7th chords moving down chromatically and a stylized melody that implies a #9 to b9 of the dominant 7th of the key (D7). While this is a more contemporary jazz sound, it is not what the composer intended.

As originally written, the melody in bar 6 has a passing diminished chord and a chromatic descending melody to match.

After I spent time acclimating to the melody and chords as written, I preferred the original for compositional reasons as is the case with most of these tunes.

In the bridge of the tune at bar 3, Van Heusen did write the parallel descending minor 7th chords with the chromatic melody that implies the #9 to b9 of the dominant of the key area:

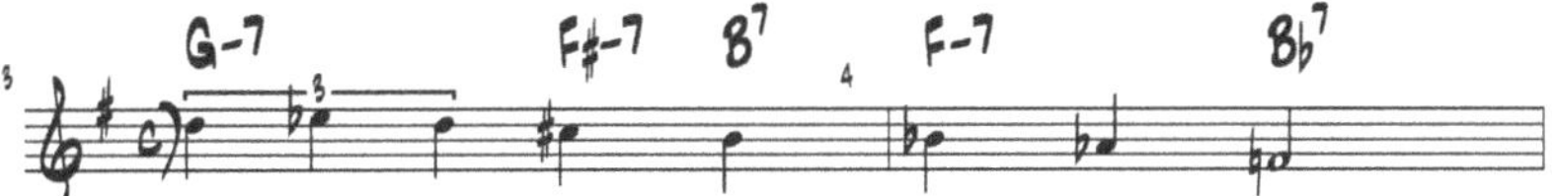

If you play the parallel minor 7ths and the #9 to b9 melody in all the A sections, it devalues that usage in the bridge and becomes redundant.

Most vocalists, especially on earlier recordings, sing the original melody in bar 6 of the A sections and their arrangers wrote the passing diminished chord that works with that melody. Here are some vocal and instrumental artists that perform bar 6 as written:

Joe Williams, Ella Fitzgerald, Billie Holiday, Thelonious Monk, Ahmad Jamal, Sarah Vaughan, Stan Kenton, Bill Charlap, Tony Bennett, Teddy Wilson, Buddy DeFranco.

Concerning fake books, some show the original, some show the stylized version. The original *Real Book* and the *Colorado Cookbook* show the stylized melody. The *Jazz Fakebook* shows the melody as originally written. And *The New Real Book Vol. I* has the stylized melody in its lead sheet but shows the original as a footnote at the bottom of the page.

Desafinado

Composed by Antônio Carlos Jobim, lyrics by Newton Mendoça, 1958
Form: A (16 bars), A' (16 bars), B (16 bars), A" (20 bars)
Standard key: F

This tune is included in the book mainly due to its quirky form. The first two A sections are each 16 bars long, but the tricky part is the key change in bar 13 of the second A section. The standard key of the tune is F, but the last four bars of the second A section modulate to the key of A. Since the bridge continues in the key of A, it's not easy to identify the start of the bridge. This complication is evident in the original *Real Book* which left out the last four bars of the second A section altogether.

Four

**Composition credited to Miles Davis, but generally considered to
be written by Eddie "Cleanhead" Vinson
Form: 32 bars - 16 with first ending, 16 with second ending
Standard Key: Eb**

There are a few spots in this tune that can be conceptualized differently depending on where you learned it. Miles' best-known recordings of the tune are from the 1954 album *Blue Haze* and the 1956 album *Workin'*. The *Blue Haze* version seems slightly ragged in a few places, and the tune, by the 1956 recording, is better defined.

There can be some disagreement as to what the chord in bar 9 is. The chords in bars 7 and 8 are Ab-7 and Db7 (ii-V in Gb). The melody in bar 9 outlines Eb major and the chords in bar 10 are F#-7 and B7 (ii-V in E) then F-7 in bar 11.

So, the voice leading of the bass notes from bar 7 through bar 11 would indicate a bass note of G in measure 9, making that chord Eb/G. Measures 13, 14, and 15 contain the same chord progression as measures 9, 10, and 11.

In the 1954 recording, the band seems to be implying more of a G-7 in bar 9, but on the 1956 recording they're playing Eb major, sometimes with a G in the bass. I prefer this as it honors the melody better than G-7.

Also on the 1954 recording, the band plays D-7b5 and G7b9 (ii-V in C minor) in bar 12:

It works nicely moving from the F-7 in bar 11, but it sets up a harmonic dead end when the G7b9 chord moves back to the Eb/G in bar 13. I prefer the simpler ii-V of F-7 in bar 11 and Bb7 in bar 12 as played on the 1956 recording:

The Sher Music *New Real Book* lead sheet of this tune lays out the alternative possibilities quite nicely.

Then there's the issue of the old original *Real Book*. It had the chord changes 3 through 6 as Bb-7, Eb7, Ab Maj 7: a ii-V-I in Ab major.

Miles' chord changes in those measures are Eb-7, Ab7, F-7. So, if you learned it from the original *Real Book*, there will be a conflict if you play the tune with players who learned it from Miles' recordings. I also prefer Miles' changes in those bars for an aesthetic reason. The Ab major key area sounds too major. Starting the second 4-bar phrase on the F-7 has much more attitude, at least to my ear.

Freddie Freeloader

Composed by Miles Davis, 1959
Form: Usually considered to be a 12-bar blues
Standard Key: Bb

The inclusion of "Freddie Freeloader" in this book is due to theoretical rather than practical considerations. "Freddie" is usually performed as a 12-bar blues, but it is my belief that Miles intended for the tune to be a 24-bar form. Let's look at some details from the original recording from 1959.

When the head of the tune is played, it is played as 12 bars with a first ending and 12 bars with a second ending. The first 12-bar statement ends with 2 bars of Ab7, and the second 12 bars ends with 2 bars of Bb7 and a different melodic cadence:

The first soloist is Wynton Kelly. When soloing and comping, Wynton consistently ends the first 12 bars with 2 bars of Ab7 and ends the second 12 bars with 1 bar of Ab7 and 1 bar of Bb7:

He plays three 24-bar choruses (or six 12-bar choruses) keeping this first ending/second ending routine intact. When Miles solos, Wynton continues the first ending/second ending routine. Miles also plays three 24-bar choruses (or six 12-bar choruses). When Coltrane solos, Wynton continues to honor the first ending/second ending routine. However, Coltrane plays five 12-bar choruses and hands it off to Cannonball. At this point, Wynton resets the routine to the first ending chords: 2 bars of Ab7 then continues the first ending/second ending routine. Cannonball plays five 12-bar choruses and stops. Paul Chambers begins his solo and Wynton again resets the first ending/second ending routine. Paul plays one 24-bar chorus (or two 12-bar choruses) and the horns come back in to play the head out.

As a practical matter, keeping track of first and second endings on this tune could be a bit fussy. I've never played the tune on a gig where anyone bothered to change endings every other 12 bars. I've had some of my student ensembles perform the tune with the intent to honor the 24-bar form, but it rarely stays intact for the whole performance. We're so used to playing 12-bar blues that it's very easy to just play the blues and disregard Miles' 24-bar form. Probably, no one in the audience would notice either.

Have Yourself A Merry Little Christmas

This song might seem like an odd one to include in this book, but I do so because it is a classic example of needing to pay attention to first, second, and third endings. Each A section ending melody begins in the fifth bar of that section with an arpeggio from the third of the I chord, and each ending is contoured differently to highlight the lyric and match the chord progression.

At the end of the first A section, the melody cadences downward and the chord progression turns around to start the second A section back on the I chord:

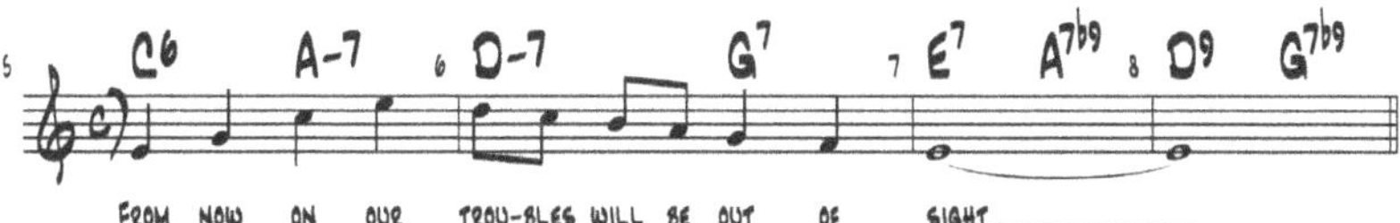

At the end of the second "A" section, the melody starts to cadence downward then resolves upward with the chord progression modulating to A minor to set up the bridge starting in F:

For the third ending, the melody climaxes by turning up, then descending a bit and resolving upward with the chord progression again modulating to A minor to set up the 4 bar tag in F:

It's a great compositional device to sequence each of the three A sections with progressively higher cadences. Note, too, the relationship between the lyrics of each ending and the contour of the melody. In the first A section the lyric is "our troubles will be out of sight" as the melody descends. In the second A section, the lyric is "our troubles will be miles away" as the melody descends then turns back upward. And, in the third A section, the lyric is "Hang a shining star upon the highest bough" as the melody ascends with the highest note in the song being on the word "star." Then the melody turns downward and back up again to ascend to "highest bough."

There are many recordings of this song (usually by younger pop artists) where the performer sings the melody of the third A section for the second ending going into the bridge as well as for the third ending. This is most likely because the more climactic third ending is more memorable and that melody also works over the chord changes modulating into the bridge, but it devalues the composer's intended compositional sequence.

There are also several sets of lyrics to this tune. The song was debuted in the movie *Meet Me in St. Louis* by Judy Garland in 1944. It's a very melancholy moment in the movie and Judy thought the original lyric was too depressing and pressed for a re-write. It was tweaked a bit for the movie, but a couple of years later, Frank Sinatra wanted to record the song and requested even more changes. Those edits led to the version most folks know today.

I Could Write A Book

Composed by Richard Rodgers and Lorenz Hart, 1940
For the musical *Pal Joey*
Form: 32 bars, 16 with first ending, 16 with second ending

If you listen to 20 recordings of this tune, you will hear 20 different sets of chord changes. The problematic part of the tune is the third 4-bar phrase of each half. The original chord changes as written by Richard Rodgers are great, but they don't lend themselves to the ii-V routines that jazz players like to navigate.

Here are the original chords in bars 9 through 12 of the 1st 1/2:

And here are the original chords in bars 9 through 12 of the 2nd 1/2:

Many players have learned this tune from the Miles Davis Quintet recording *Cookin'*, 1956. His rhythm section on this recording (Red Garland on piano and Paul Chambers on bass) have reharmonized these bars. In addition, their reharmonization is not succinct in that they don't seem to clearly define the progression in each of these 4-bar sections. In bar 8 of each 1/2, they play a ii-V into the A-7 in bar 9.

Here is what I believe they are playing in bars 9 through 12 of the 1st 1/2:

Here is what I believe they are playing in bars 9 through 12 of the 2nd 1/2:

When studying multiple recordings of this tune, I found all sorts of combinations of the above examples and no two alike.

On *Tony Bennett Sings 10 Rodgers & Hart Songs*, 1976, the arrangement uses the original C/E to Ab7/Eb walkdown in both the first and second halves of the tune.

I listened to a couple of recordings of George Shearing playing the tune. One is *Satin Brass*, 1959. This recording is the George Shearing Quintet with a studio orchestra. Another is *Mel & George "Do" World War II*, 1990, a record with Mel Torme and George Shearing. On *Satin Brass*, Shearing honors the original chord progression in bars 9 through 12 of both halves of the tune. On the recording with Mel Torme, Shearing honors the original chord progression in bars 9 through 12 of the first half, but does the A- in bar 9 of the second half a la Red Garland from the Miles recording.

On *Anita O'Day and Billy May Swing Rodgers and Hart*, 1960, Billy uses the same approach as the recording by Mel Torme and George Shearing: original chords in the 1st half and Miles' chords in the second half.

Scott Hamilton, on his album *I Could Write a Book*, 2013, uses the Miles chord changes on both halves.

So, bars 9 through 12 of both halves of this tune are somewhat of a jump ball. The turnarounds in bars 13 through 16 of both halves can be quite varied as well. When this tune is called on a gig, you just need to know the possibilities and keep your ears open, unless the band is working from an agreed upon set of changes.

I tend to prefer a hybrid approach to this tune. For bars 9 through 12 in the first half:

For those bars in the second half, I use the changes from Miles' recording. The change to A- on bar 9 of the second half gives it a nice contrast from the first half.

I Remember You

**Composed by Victor Schertzinger with lyrics by Johnny Mercer, 1941
Form: A (8 bars) A (8 bars) B (8 bars) A (12 bars)
Standard Key: F**

This tune has a 12-bar last A section, so it has a written-in tag. A common mistake in this section is to go to the wrong key at the beginning of the written tag. In bars 4 and 5 of the last A, there should be a minor ii-V-i into the ii chord of the key:

I've heard these two bars played as a ii-V-I into the IV chord of the key:

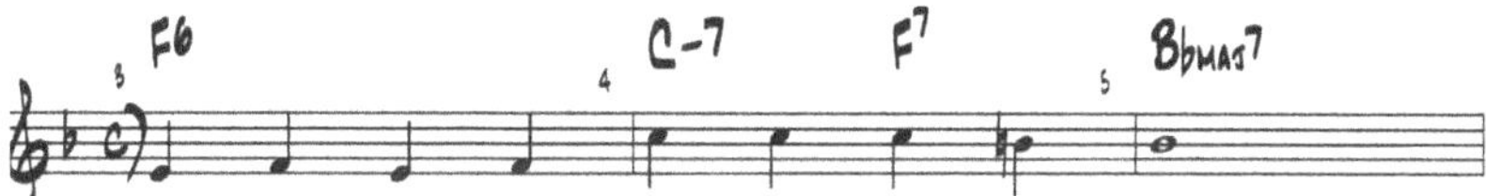

It works well enough that way but just doesn't seem to have harmonic gravity of the minor key. Again, the composer knew best.

I Thought About You

Composed by Jimmy Van Heusen with lyrics by Johnny Mercer, 1939
Form: 32 bars - 16 with first ending, 16 with second ending
Standard Key: F

In this tune, there is a small bit of melody that needs attention. In bars 15 and 16 of the 1st half, the melody is written like this:

It is very easy to hear those two measures as a sequence of 3rds and perform it like this:

In bar 16, the original G-A-A melody makes more sense as the final note of the phrase is the 13th of the C7 chord. If you sequence the 3rds, the melody ends on the 7th which, to my ear, is a less consonant or resolved sound.

Van Heusen knew what worked best.

In Your Own Sweet Way

Composed by Dave Brubeck, 1955
Form (Dave Brubeck version): A (8 bars) A (8 bars)
B (8 bars) A (10 bars)
Form (Miles Davis version): A (8 bars) A (8 bars) B (8 bars)
A (8 bars) C (8 bars)

This tune is complicated by the fact that Dave Brubeck wrote it, but Miles Davis had the more famous recording of it. And Miles' version is significantly different than Dave's.

When looking at the timeline for this tune, it appears that Miles recorded the song before Brubeck's recording was released. Miles recorded his version with two different groups - one in March of 1956 and one in May of 1956. Brubeck's first recording of the tune was released in July of 1956. So, it seems Miles probably heard the tune at a festival or in a club and brought it to his group via his memory of the tune.

I learned the tune by ear from Miles' recording, as did most players of the pre-*Real Book* era. It was considerably later that I studied Brubeck's version and began to realize the differences.

Brubeck wrote the tune in Eb (with a 2-bar cadence at the end on Eb-). Miles' version omits the Eb6 chord on the 3rd and 4th beats of measure 8 in the first two A sections and cadences the first two A sections on Bb9, effectively moving the key center to Bb. Also, Miles' A sections melody ends on E natural instead of F, making the #11 of the Bb9 chord the melody.

Brubeck's bridge starts in D major, Miles' in D minor. There are a couple subtle chord substitutions in the bridge as well.

After the last A section, Brubeck cadences to a 2-bar Eb-chord, but Miles goes to an 8-bar pedal Ab vamp.

These differences are important because it makes the tune difficult to call on a gig or jam session. You'll never know which details of what version the players are going to use.

When I have questions about melody or chords on a tune, I find that when I study what the composer originally wrote I almost always prefer that. And that is the case for this tune.

For a good side-by-side comparison of the two versions, check out *The New Real Book, Vol. II*. It has both Dave Brubeck's and Miles Davis' versions completely notated.

Suggested listening:
Find Brubeck's live recording of this tune from Newport, July 1956, with Paul Desmond soloing. Desmond is brilliant.

Just Friends

**Composed by John Klenner and Sam M. Lewis, 1931
Form: 32 bars, 16 with first ending, 16 with second ending
First hit recording by vocalist Russ Columbo with the Leonard Joy
Orchestra, 1932**

The first and second halves of this tune are similar, and that similarity has led to a very common error. In bar 11 of each half, the ending for that half is defined. If you're playing the tune in the key of G, the chords at bar 11 in the first half should be one bar of G Maj 7 and one bar of E-7. Also, the melody sequences down from bars 9 and 10, then proceeds to the last four bars of the first half which function as a turnaround to set up the second half of the tune.

In the second half, the chords at bar 11 should be 2 beats of F# half diminished, 2 beats of B7b9, and one bar of E-7 and the melody sequences up to set up the last four bars of the tune to cadence on the G Maj chord.

In other words, Bar 11 in the first half is I to vi in G major but in the second half, it's ii-V-I in E minor.

The common error is that instrumentalists, instead of playing bars 11 and 12 of the first and second halves as written, tend to play bars 11 and 12 of the second half both times. *The Tom Lord Jazz Discography* lists over 700 recordings of this song. I've listened to many versions of this song and a large percentage of them play the tune this way. I can only surmise that the subtle key change in bar 11 of the second half of the tune is more interesting and/or memorable than bars 11 and 12 in the first half. So, players may tend to hear the second half of the tune and disregard the first half.

The downside of this is that it ignores the composer's intent to delineate between first and second endings of the tune which devalues the harmonic and melodic lift intended for the second half of the tune.

Performances that reflect the original composition in bar 11 include Charlie Spivak, Sarah Vaughan, Sonny Stitt, Phil Woods, and most older orchestra and vocal recordings.

Misty

Composed by Erroll Garner, 1954
Lyrics added later by Johnny Burke
Form: A A B A, 8 bars per section
Standard Key: Eb

The bridge of this tune is complicated by several issues. I have recordings of Erroll Garner playing the tune in the keys of Ab, Db, C, and Eb. He also played the bridge with different chord changes at different times in his career. For purposes of analysis, I will relate all variations to the key of Eb, which seems to be the key most players use.

On his original recording and earlier performances, he used these chords starting in bar 5 of the bridge:

In later recordings and performances, his chords starting in bar 5 of the bridge evolved into this:

Also complicating the understanding of this bridge are a couple of commonly used lead sheets that have other approaches to the bridge. The old original *Real Book* has this for bar 5 of the bridge:

The New Real Book, Vol. I has this for those 4 bars:

The D7 to F7 in bar 6 of both lead sheets seems rather angular to me and the turnaround in bar 7 of the old *Real Book* version seems contrived. I can't find any recordings of Garner playing the bridge as written in either of those books. For those reasons, I prefer Garner's later version of the bridge (2nd example above). This is the bridge that seems to have become standard usage.

Night And Day

Composed by Cole Porter, 1932
Form: A B A B C B (6 eight bar sections)
Standard Key: Eb

Cole Porter frequently wrote subtle differences into repeated sections of his tunes. "Night And Day" is a classic example of this. To really know this tune you should be familiar with the lyric and listen to recordings of the tune by pop vocalists of the American Songbook era.

The A sections have slightly different melodies that can be discerned by studying the lyric. The second A section has more syllables, so the melody has more notes and a slightly different contour. The G to F# half step in these phrases sometimes gets as G to F. The F# is original.

Bar 6 of the first A section:

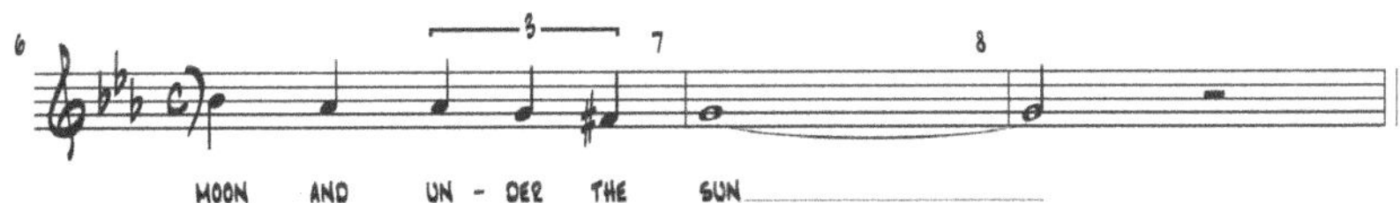

Bar 6 of the second A section:

The first two B sections are alike, having a descending melody in bars 4 and 5:

But the last B section has an ascending interval in bar 4 before continuing the descending melody, and then cadences on the tonic rather than the dominant:

There is also some disagreement regarding the first chord of the song. Cole Porter wrote a bVI Maj7 as the first chord (BMaj7 in the key of Eb). Since jazz musicians have a fondness for ii-Vs, the first chord is often performed as a ii half diminished (F-7b5 in the key of Eb).

Softly, As In A Morning Sunrise

Composed by Sigmund Romberg, lyrics by Oscar Hammerstein II, 1928
Form: A A B A, 8 bars per section
Standard Key: C minor

The issue for this tune is how the last 3 bars of each A section
are played. Knowledge of the lyrics in these 2 measures will clarify.
Here is the written melody with the lyric from bars 5, 6, and 7 of
the first A section:

Here is an example of how those bars are often misplayed:

Note that the second example doesn't fit the lyric. Also, the
tune was written and performed originally as a tango in the 1928
operetta *The New Moon*. The eighth note rest on beat one of bar 6
is more idiomatic to the tango than would be a downbeat, as in the
second example.

When played like the second example, bars 6 and 7 just sound
like an incorrect statement of "A Night In Tunisia."

Song For My Father

**Composed by Horace Silver, 1964
Form: A A B, 8 bars per section**

While not a complicated tune, you need to be aware of the form: A A B. I've played this tune with musicians who are fooled by the B section - hearing it as a bridge that needs to be followed by a third A section. That last A section does not exist. The head is usually played twice, which results in several A sections back-to-back. This can be particularly confusing, so you must remember to restart the form in your mind when you finish the B section to go to the top of the tune.

If, on the head, your melody player plays A A B A then stops, this can result in much confusion about where the band is in the form. And the band can have a hard time recovering.

Here are examples of some other tunes with uncommon forms that need attention.

"Little Sunflower" (Freddie Hubbard) is A (16 bars) B (16 bars) A (16 bars). The 16-bar A sections are modal - 16 bars of D minor. The bridge is Eb major and D major. So, it's very easy to get lost in that ocean of D minor if you're not paying close attention to the form. You need to be aware of the 4 and 8 bar phrases.

"The Night Has A Thousand Eyes" is A A B (all 16 bars sections)
"I'll Remember April" is A B A (all 16 bar sections)
"You Go To My Head" is A A B A C (all 8 bar sections)

That's All

Composed by Alan Brandt and Bob Haymes, 1952
Form: A A B A, 8 bars per section
Standard Key: Bb

Early in my career I played with many lounge/jazz pianists and this tune was a crowd favorite, especially to close the gig at the end of the night. I was never a huge fan of this tune, so I was fine not playing it for years. But recently, an ensemble I was teaching requested putting this tune in their repertoire. So, I consulted The *New Real Book, Vol. II* and discovered why I had trouble liking this song. The "jazzy" chord progressions that have become standard usage for "That's All" don't work very well with the melody. While the melody is pretty and works by itself and the standard usage chord progressions sound nice, the combination of the two create dissonances that are hard to make musical.

Here is what you will probably hear played for bars 3 through 6 of the A sections:

If you play BbMaj7 to Eb9 in measure 3, there's a D natural in the melody that rubs against the 7th of the Eb9. In measure 5, if you use the descending progression that starts on E-7b5, there's a G natural in the melody that doesn't work with the Eb-7 on beats 3 and 4. Also, there's a Bb in the melody of bar 6 on beat 3. If you're playing the G7 chord there, it must be altered to accommodate the Bb, creating some harsh dissonance.

Here is another common chord progression for bars 3 and 4:

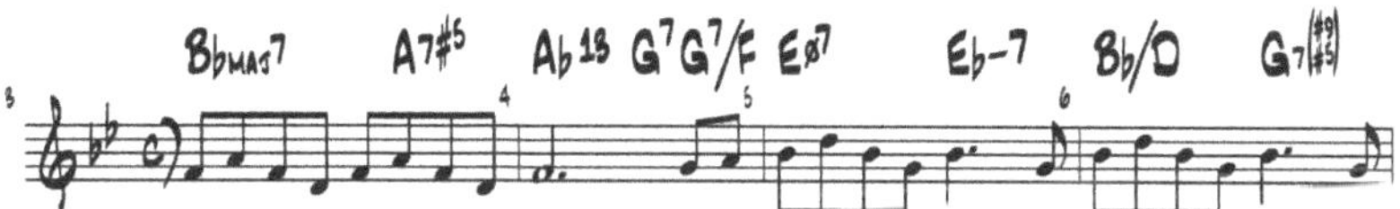

This involves dominant 7th chords descending by 1/2 step. The melody in measure 3 has F naturals and D naturals in it. So, if you play the A7 on beat 3 of the third measure you must alter the 5th and you have the 11th (D natural on beat 4) up against the third of the chord (C#). Again, some dissonance.

After playing this tune a couple times in class, I decided to do some research and listened to some early recordings of the song. The original hit seems to be by Nat Cole (1957). It's a beautiful arrangement by Nelson Riddle and the chord progression contains none of the dissonant rubs that are common usage. Then I found a recording by Ben Webster with Oscar Peterson. Again, really nice chord changes that complement the melody. I took this set of chords to class and all players in the ensemble agreed they wanted to use those chords.

Here is the progression used by Nelson Riddle and Oscar Peterson:

There are other ways to make the tune work. Since the "jazzy" changes and the original melody do not agree very well, one or the other needs a little alteration. There are a couple of recordings by Gene Harris with Ray Brown where they use the descending dominant 7th chords in bars 3 and 4. To facilitate this, Gene interprets the melody (in his usual blues style) to play across those changes.

Ray Brown Trio: *Soular Energy*, 1984
The Red Hot Ray Brown Trio, 1985

There's also a later Sarah Vaughan recording where she sings the original melody against the jazzier changes, but it works because it's done at a considerably brighter tempo, so the dissonances move by quickly and Sarah knows how to finesse that melody to make it work.

Sarah Vaughan: *Crazy and Mixed Up*, 1982

The Song Is You

Composed by Jerome Kern and Oscar Hammerstein II, 1932
Form: A A B A, 16 bars per section
Standard Key: C

The thing to watch in this tune is the melodic and harmonic differences between the A sections. The melody of each A section is slightly different. The first 2 measures of the third A section sequence up and then the tune modulates up with a ii-V-I in the key of F to give the tune a sense of finality.

First 4 bars of first and second A sections:

First 4 bars of the third A section:

Also, measures 6 and 7 of the second and third A sections sequence upward, while the chord progression cadences in the key of C. In the second A section, this cadence sets up the modulation into the bridge and in the third A section it ends the tune.

From bar 5 of the first A section:

From bar 5 of the second and third A sections:

There are a lot of possibilities for chord changes on this tune. If you listen to 10 recordings of the song, you will probably hear 10 different ideas of what the chords are. My main point for including this tune in the book is to understand that the ii-V-I in F should only happen in the last A section.

A lot of folks use the ii-V-I in F in the second A section, especially when soloing. Maybe they get bored of loitering in C and want to do something different in the second A section. But that devalues the harmonic forward motion that gives the last A section its sense of "ending". So, resist the temptation to play the third A section twice.

Well You Needn't

This one is complicated in that almost no one plays it like Monk wrote it. If you listen to five recordings of this tune, you will probably hear five different ideas of how the tune goes. Between the original *Real Book* lead sheet and Miles Davis' well-known recordings of the tune, a lot has gone sideways.

Let's start with the first two notes of the melody. Monk's first notes are a G# pickup to an A on the downbeat:

Many lead sheets and recordings have the first two notes as B to C, which also alters the following arpeggio:

My guess would be that this may have evolved because of the range of Bb instruments. The original notes on a Bb horn would be Bb to B natural – bottom of the range for tenor sax and fairly low for trumpet. Charlie Rouse, however, played the low Bb with Monk.

Next is the tonality of the A sections. Monk plays Major 6 chords on the A sections – F6 and Gb6. This is defined nicely by what he plays with his left hand on the A sections of the *Monk's Music* recording of this tune. Dominant 7 chords are used on the A sections by many players instead of the Major 6 chords. The bridge of the tune is a Mixolydian modality so, to my ear, if you play the Dominant 7 chords on the A sections as well, the whole tune becomes Mixolydian, and you lose the change up of tonality that Monk intended for the bridge.

Now let's consider the bridge of the tune. Monk's bridge starts on Db7. When Miles recorded it, his bridge started on G7, which dictated that he plays a different melody than Monk wrote. This may have happened because Miles was playing the tune as he remembered it from hearing it live by other players and not referencing Monk's recording.

As a result of these stylizations, when this tune is called on a gig I always ask, "Monk's bridge or Miles'?"

The old original *Real Book* has Miles' melody (with the wrong rhythm), dominant seventh chords on the A section, and Miles' bridge.

The new Hal Leonard *Real Book* has Monk's melody on the A sections and Monk's bridge but kept the dominant seventh chords in the A sections.

Sher's *New Real Book* has the Major 6 chords on the A sections but kept Miles' melody and bridge and shows Monk's bridge as an alternate.

The *Colorado Cookbook* has authentic versions of the tune by both artists.

Versions of the tune played more like Monk's:

Thelonious Monk: *Monk's Music,* 1957
Cannonball Adderley: *The Cannonball Adderley Quintet Plus,* 1961
Phil Woods and Franco D'Andrea: *Our Monk,* 1994

A stylization that honors the original composition:
Sphere: *Sphere On Tour,* 1988

What Is This Thing Called Love

Composed by Cole Porter, 1929
Form: A A B A, 8 bars per section
Standard Key: C

Cole Porter often writes subtle but important variances in similar sections of his tunes. The melody in the first 2 bars of each A section of this tune needs attention. The number of syllables in the lyrics will inform regarding number of notes in the melody. The first 2 bars of the song state the title in the lyric:

The first 2 bars of the second A section have a lyric with a different number of syllables and Porter alters the melody to accommodate:

In the last A section, the lyric and the melody are different again (note also that it has 3 pickup notes instead of one):

Many instrumentalists will use these three 2-bar phrases interchangeably, but that is not what the composer intended. Knowing the lyrics to tunes will clarify the written melody.

When Lights Are Low

Composed by Benny Carter and Spencer Williams, 1936
Form: A A B A, 8 bars per section
Standard Key: Eb

The bridge to this tune got lost somewhere along the way. When I was first exposed to "When Lights Are Low," I had heard Miles' recording and then played it a few times at jam sessions, and I remember thinking that the bridge was not very inventive. When Miles Davis recorded it for *Blue Haze* in 1953, he simply repeated the A section up a fourth as the bridge. Years later I discovered Benny Carter's original bridge which is a fairly complicated series of key changes around the cycle of fourths. That has much more substance and sounds more like a Carter composition. All recordings I've listened to that predate the Miles recording use Carter's bridge. Vocal recordings use the Carter bridge since the lyric is tied to that original bridge melody. After Miles' 1953 recording, many instrumental versions by major jazz artists use the simpler Davis bridge. This is indicative of the power of a recording by one artist to alter many players' conception of a tune.

The original *Real Book Vol. II* has the Davis bridge, and the *New Real Book Vol. III* includes both versions.

Recordings that use the original bridge:
Any recording by Benny Carter
Lionel Hampton, 1939 (Benny Carter is arranger
    and alto player)
George Shearing, 1952
Cal Tjader: *Our Blues*, 1957
Billy Taylor: *One for Fun*, 1959
Howard Roberts: *Color Him Funky*, 1963
Jaki Byard: *Parisian Solos*, 1971
Kenny Barron: *Green Chimneys*, 1983
Red Mitchell: *Remembering Red*, 1991

Oscar Peterson and Benny Green: *Oscar & Benny*, 1997
  Miles' bridge is used by Oscar on all other recordings
  I could find
Pete Christlieb with the Lori Mechem Quartet:
  Live at the Jazz Cave, 2006

You Took Advantage of Me

Composed by Richard Rodgers and Lorenz Hart, 1928
Form: A A B A, 8 bars per section
Standard Key: Eb

The opening statement of this melody rarely gets performed as written. The first two notes of the melody are a unison 5th scale degree, making the melody:

It is commonly performed:

When you compare the opening statement of the melody to the 3rd and 4th bar restatement of the motif, the original makes sense as the statement in bar 3 starts with the same unison 5th:

The first bar of the melody probably mutated to 5 3 1 7 b7 because it is a bit more melodic and easier to articulate.

Fake books are inconclusive about the opening measure. Some have it as originally written (original *Real Book*), some have it as it has been popularized, and some have it written both ways with the 3rd scale degree on the second 8th note parenthesized (*The Standards Real Book* from Sher Music).

Artists who perform the melody as written:
Paul Whiteman w/Bing Crosby & Trio, 1928
Ella Fitzgerald: *Ella Sings the Rodgers and Hart Song Book*, 1956
Benny Carter: *Cosmopolite*, 1955
Teddy Wilson: *For Quiet Lovers*, 1955
Benny Goodman: *The Sextet Sessions*, 1947

SUMMARY

Now that we've slogged through some analyses of these tunes, let's consider how to apply this analytical process to other tunes you may want to clarify. Here are some guidelines:

1. Do your research. Versions of songs often fall into one of three categories:

- What the composer wrote
- What has become standard usage
- Any other variation involving chord substitutions or interpreted melody that has become popular

Trace the song to its earliest performances, preferably by the composer or by artists with whom the composer was working. Knowing what the composer intended is valuable. Virtually every time I have had questions about standard usage that caused some cognitive dissonance, referencing what the composer wrote cleared up the conflict. Composers wrote the songs as they did for a reason.

2. Study the lyrics. Knowing the lyrics will inform a lot about the melody. The number of syllables in a phrase will tell you how many notes are in that phrase. Knowing the lyrics can also tell you about the contour of the melody, which may delineate subtle differences in A sections of a tune (e.g., "What Is This Thing Called Love"). Knowing the lyric will help you understand the meter and the accents of a song, which notes are to be emphasized, played long, played short, etc. Knowing the lyrics will help you understand the sentiment of a tune so that you can determine an appropriate tempo or style in which to perform the song.

3. Know the form of the song. There are some common forms such as A A B A, 32-bar tune with a first and second half, and 12-bar blues. When you get into less common forms such as A B A, A B B, A A B A C, you need to pay attention to the form and not get lost.

4. Take all lead sheets with a grain of salt. Every lead sheet is someone's idea of how the song goes. If you look at five lead sheets for a given song, you will probably see five different ideas of how the song should be performed.

5. Study multiple versions of a song. Listen to multiple recordings by artists you like. Look at multiple lead sheets from different sources. Contrast and compare the differences in these versions.

This book is not meant to be a comprehensive review of Great American Songbook or Jazz Standard compositions. It is a primer on how to deal with the subtle intricacies of the literature. What makes a great doctor or a great lawyer (or, for that matter, any highly skilled professional)? It requires a deep knowledge of the literature and science of their fields as well as a talent for creative problem solving. The same is true for musicians, especially in the jazz idiom where there is so much freedom for interpretation. The analyses I have presented here are not simply about what is "right" or "wrong" regarding how to play these tunes but knowing the possibilities while honoring the composition.

Once you have gone through this process, you can make educated decisions as to how you would like to perform the tune. This will also prepare you for any variations of that tune that may happen in real-time performance.

Acknowledgements

There are many people who made it possible for me to learn and play the music I have enjoyed for my entire career. I would like to thank them and the friends who made this book happen.

Dr. David Baker and Dr. John Spicknall who broadened my knowledge of the American Songbook and exposed me to classic jazz compositions and artists during my college days.

Robert Goodlett, John Clayton, Frank Gallagher, and Arni Egilsson for not only being great bassists but great teachers as well.

The many seasoned musicians who took me under their wing as a young player and trusted me to grow into their musical world.

Numerous musical cohorts who share my love of this literature and love performing it with me.

My faculty associates and students from Vanderbilt's Blair School of Music and the Nashville Jazz Workshop who encouraged the writing of the book.

Liz Johnson for editing this book and wrangling me with deadlines to get the book done.

Linda Johnson at Johnson Desktop Publishing for the book layout.

Brian Parker of Parker Designs for the beautiful cover and graphics.

And my wife, Lori Mechem, for sharing my love of this music, inspiring me to write about it, and listening to me complain about wrong melodies and chord changes for over 35 years.